LETTERS

MICHAEL GILBRIDE

Leda and the Swan
By William Butler Yeats

A sudden blow: the great wings beating still
Above the staggering girl, her thighs caressed
By the dark webs, her nape caught in his bill,
He holds her helpless breast upon his breast.

How can those terrified vague fingers push
The feathered glory from her loosening thighs?
And how can body, laid in that white rush,
But feel the strange heart beating where it lies?

A shudder in the loins engenders there
The broken wall, the burning roof and tower
And Agamemmnon dead.
Being so caught up,
So mastered by the brute blood of the air,
Did she put on his knowledge with his power
Before the indifferent beak could let her drop?

ISBN: 978-1-09832-158-1

1

June 10, 2020

There were times when I wondered and even meditated upon my love of letters—both writing and receiving letters. I thought of my father who I came to understand when I was very young worked for the post office. Maybe subconsciously, I associated receiving letters as gifts from him, from his work. Then there was my mother's family in Ireland. My grandmother lived with us in our house in Bay Ridge, Brooklyn, and before, her mother lived with us until she was ninety-nine. She had come to America as an indentured servant and worked almost every day of her life until she just could not work anymore. The way the family in America kept in touch with the family in Ireland through the 1950s and 1960s was by means of letters. I can remember sitting on the stoop of our house in Bay Ridge with my mother and some of the family, and the task of reading the letters from Ireland as though reading a proclamation fell to me, as I could read well and didn't need glasses. I loved to read the letters from Ireland that seemed so far away; the letters handwritten placed in envelopes that folded into postal mail. I came to have a pen pal in Ireland, a cousin Terry whose father was a university professor. My mother told me that when I was young, they had visited our home in Brooklyn en route to Chicago and I gave Terry my toy fire engine. It wasn't until the year 2006 that I would again come face to face with Terry in Dublin as I traveled there to introduce my wife. Fr. Peter, the Holy Ghost Father from Kimmage Manor, who came to New York each summer since I was about thirteen, sought to befriend me. He managed to encourage the family on both sides of the Atlantic to keep touch with each other. I had traveled to Ireland in 1989, and Fr. Peter took me through the west of Ireland to Yeat's grave and the mountain Ben Bulben. He was a wonderful host. I said a rosary with his mother Kitty McEntire, who was a hundred years old and had been a midwife in the Great War and traveled around by bicycle. Fr. Peter's house, where his mother resided, had a lake out back and he had a boat.

He grew potatoes and we had to put on Wellington boots so that we could get in the little boat. I remember when we were out on the lake, I had never felt so far away from the hustle and bustle of New York City. Fr. Peter's mother's husband had died, and his brother, who had been a farmer out in Oregon, had come back and married her. Fr. Peter was to me definitely an honorary if not a "de facto" American besides being a consummate Irish priest. Fr. Peter had been a missionary in what was originally Tanganikya, which then became Tanzania. He was famous for having lived under Mount Kilimanjaro. He could say his prayers in English, Latin, and Swahili. Peter, as the family called him, would visit me every summer. He would stay in the little room on the second floor in the apartment my grandmother and aunt shared. The room was where my great-grandmother had died when she was ninety-nine with the family all around her. My own mother later told everyone she could see my great-grandmother's soul depart her body. I had struck up a correspondence with Peter and would write to him, mostly about being gay and feeling rejected by the church. Peter would always encourage me and would always answer my letters.

My cousin Terry, whose father was a university professor, had been diagnosed as schizophrenic, and though I never went into it with Peter, during counseling at Columbia University, I too had been diagnosed as schizophrenic. Though I had many, many issues with the Catholic Church, not the least of which was the fact that many priests I knew were sexual, I came to love and respect Fr. Peter. He had taught at Blackrock College and had trouble with students. But, each summer, we would get together, no matter what. We'd talk about family, about religion, about politics. He always treated me with

Michael Gilbride at the grave of William Butler Yeats – 1989

2

respect. We would always go to a nice restaurant and share some wine. I was always grateful to Peter for letting me stay at Kimmage Manor in 1989 and then taking me to the west of Ireland. As a side story. My brother's family had asked me to deliver a chalice to a Fr. Gallagher in Ireland in memory of Dr. John the dentist. I said I would try. I was stopped at Customs and they found the chalice and charged me $80 for taxes. Fr. Peter who was waiting for me asked, "What are you bringing a chalice to Ireland for?" "it's like taking coals to Newcastle." But we did locate Fr. Gallagher, and he was a beekeeper. He gave me jars of honey to bring to everyone in the States. I wondered about Peter telling me not to "look up" my cousin Terry in Ireland. He told me to leave Terry alone because he "takes tablets for his mind." I never told Peter about my own diagnosis being the same as Terry's, but wondered to myself about the family in Ireland keeping Terry hidden. When I did meet Terry, I learned he had three children and a wife, who was a solicitor. He worshipped with both Moslems and Jews, and went to Catholic Church as well. He worked for the National Health System. I had just graduated from Brooklyn College and was a Certified School Psychologist in New York. I was filled with righteous indignation for both Terry and myself—the schizophrenics of the family. Separated by the Atlantic Ocean, but I guess united by some genetic mutation in my mother's family line. Fr. Peter introduced me to some cousins up in the north of Ireland, they were young. Caroline and Patricia and Eamon and their parents Mai and John Joe and their family dog Skippy. They lived on a farm in Fermanagh. Much later in life Patricia would graduate from Cambridge University with a doctoral degree in Psychology, and she told me that when she was young and they visited Terry's family, he always had to stay in his bedroom and never could come out to socialize with the family. So my fears were true that Terry had been kept in isolation and withdrawn from the family matrix. At this point, there is another story that I must tell. When I was about eighteen, I would write letters to Terry from my dorm room at Columbia University. As I said, I had only met Terry in New York when I was a child, and did not remember him. But I was intent on telling Terry that I was gay, and that if I was ever in Ireland I would like to sleep with him. When I wrote that, all communications from Ireland stopped and I never knew what happened. But much later, in Terry's study, in Ireland, he told me that his father had intercepted the letter and read what I had written. Terry told me there was a mini-crisis in the family in Ireland and that Fr. Peter was summoned and asked about me and what I was up to. Terry told me, to my surprise, that Fr. Peter "stood up" for me and that this was no great deal. Peter defended me before the family in Ireland whom I had never met.

So my love of writing and receiving letters has gotten me into trouble and caused consternation in my own mind and yet I still love to receive handwritten notes and letters. As I sit writing this, in my Bay Ridge home, I have recently come across a letter I received from a friend at Columbia University when I was an undergraduate. Her name was Val Pinsky and she was related to the anthropologist Franz Boas. We spent a Christmas vacation at her family's cabin in the Berkshires in Massachusetts. Val would regale me with stories of Cultural Anthropology and Margaret Meade and the Museum of Natural History. But I never forgot that Val, in a quiet moment in all my undergraduate sexual confusion, told me that her father was gay. I loved her for it. In the 1980s, I was living in a basement apartment in Bay Ridge and teaching at a very small Polish Catholic school in Brooklyn. I had heard that Val had gone to do her doctoral work at Cambridge. What the heck! I wrote Val a letter and it was more or less just to say "hi" and stay in touch. I remember vividly I just wrote on the envelope: "Val Pinsky—Cambridge University." Thinking to myself I am just a hopeless romantic and the letter would have about the same chance as a note in a bottle tossed into the ocean. I went on with my teaching. A few weeks later to my

3

Astonishment I received a letter from Val that she was finishing up her doctoral dissertation and hoped to be at the Smithsonian soon. I still keep that letter as an almost magical letter. I never knew what happened to Val after that, but another instance of my "thing" with letters.

Some letters and their envelopes I keep in my bedroom. After all these years, they have touched me in ways I cannot still express. While cleaning my bedroom one week, I found a letter from Professor Philip Pechukas written on Columbia University stationery. Professor Pechukas was a Chemistry Professor at Columbia. Although I never took chemistry, Professor Pechukas was important to me in another way. When I applied to Columbia in 1972, I wanted to write. I went through all the interviews and did really well on the SATs. But my friend Tim was a year ahead of me and was already at Columbia. He took over the dean's office shortly after I applied, during Nixon's invasion of Cambodia and the student uprisings. He photocopied my application in the dean's office and the responses of the professors' impressions of me as an applicant to Columbia. Professor Pechukas wrote: "He can write, we should definitely take him." But the letter I came across from Professor Pechukas was written in November 1990. I had read in the papers as I lived in my basement apartment that Professor Pechukas's daughter had been tragically killed in a car accident in Brooklyn. I had never met Professor Pechukas, and still have never met him, but wanted to extend my sympathy to him at the loss of his daughter Fiona. I remember I said that I was told he was friends with a priest who had sex with me, Fr. Ronald Petroski, and that Fr. Ron was friends with my friend Tim and me and that Professor Pechukas had given me a high rating when I applied to Columbia. Professor Pechukas responded with a wonderfully warm letter to me tell me they "buried Fiona in Wellfleet on Cape Cod, at sunset under a cloudless sky by the base of an evergreen tree … in a cemetery without gates or walls and appropriately full of prematurely dead kids from when that was more often the fate of children."

Of course, what Tim had done in copying my application and letting me know what my rater thought of me was completely against the rules. It happened in 1972. Later, there were laws passed about privacy with regards to college applications. I often wondered if I had grounds for a suit against Columbia University.

In 1976, I took a leave from study at Columbia and went to live with my gay friend and lover Gerald in San Francisco. Before I left, I started a friendship and a correspondence with a poet, Allen Ginsberg. He wrote to me at Gerald's apartment in San Francisco and asked me if I would like to work with his lover and poet Peter Orlovsky. When I got to San Francisco, I met on the street the poet Robert Duncan who was looking for a French laundry to do his shirts. Before leaving New York, I had also met and stayed with the poet John Giorno, who was also a Columbia alumnus. Reading Allen's letter in San Francisco inspired me to want to come back to New York and work with Peter Orlovsky on his manuscript. I typed the entire manuscript for his first book of poetry. But again it was a magical sort of letter that I read with Gerald in San Francisco. It said I should "invent myself by myself." I went to a concert of the "Jefferson Airplane" at Berkeley that summer. And my grandmother had given me a gold watch that she had engraved with my name and birthdate. At the concert, I met an interesting guy who was going to the University of Chicago. His name was Joel Jaffer, and he had a car. We enjoyed the concert together but maybe the next day I realized I had lost my gold watch that my grandmother had given me. I ended up going back to New York at the end of the summer, having remained in

4

Psychoanalysis with Gerald's analyst all summer. Near the end of the summer, Gerald proposed marriage to me under the eucalyptus trees on the campus of Berkeley. It was the summer of the Symbionese Liberation Army and Patty Hearst. I told Gerald that I didn't feel we should marry, because he already had his degree from Berkeley and I was going back to New York, hoping to finish my degree at Columbia. I asked if we could wait until we are on more equal footing. Little did I know when I got back to New York and Columbia, the dean refused to allow me back at school because he said I had gone to California and taken drugs. Actually, I had gone to California, stayed in therapy, taken a few valium, and seriously considered a marriage proposal. Later, I would think as times and laws changed, Columbia would definitely be in line for a lawsuit these days, not permitting two gay students time off to figure out whether they should marry. We really were in therapy together and marriage is a reason to take some time from studies. But nonetheless, I never returned to Columbia.

As for the lost watch, I thought why not contact the University of Chicago and see if they could get me an address for my friend from the Jefferson Airplane concert. I contacted the University of Chicago and they provided me with an address for Joel. I wrote to him and sure enough he had found my grandmother's gold watch when cleaning his car. He mailed me the watch and I was ecstatic. Another magic letter. But that was not the end of the story with Joel. I tried to call him to thank him and spoke to his mother, who told me she and his father were concerned about Joel as he was schizophrenic. Bingo! Another part of the puzzle. I never heard from Joel again but still have his letters in my dresser drawer.

When I returned to Columbia in September 1975, the Department of English was about to go into mourning because of the death of a University Professor. In November of that year, I saw my advisor Professor Michael Rosenthal be a pallbearer for Professor Lionel Trilling at St. Paul's Chapel. Many thought the golden years of Columbia producing writers would die. Besides introducing myself to Allen

Ginsberg at Loeb Student Center at NYU before I went to San Francisco for the summer of 1976, I wanted to meet the Episcopal Bishop of New York, Paul Moore, who was at The Cathedral Church of Saint John the Divine. Because my experience had been that Roman Catholic priests had sexual relations with men and then were simply not honest about it, I was determined to become an Episcopalian or Anglican. Ostensibly, I had been moved by reading a Howard Fast book *April Morning*. So I made an appointment with Bishop Moore and explained my situation. I was living on Cathedral Parkway with two friends and roommates, Tim and Ellen.. Tim also had been raped by Roman Catholic priests. After a few meetings with Bishop Moore, he suggested I speak to a Jesuit, Fr. Herbert Rogers, S.J., and an assistant bishop at the Cathedral, Bishop Walter Dennis. Bishop Moore and I got together in his apartment at the Cathedral; he took me to bed, and I had mixed feelings. He told me that if anyone asked, I should not say who he was but just say I went to bed with a "tall Episcopalian." I thought, well at least Episcopal priests and bishops can honestly have sex, but this was basically the same situation that existed with Roman Catholic priests. When I got to San Francisco, apart from Allen Ginsberg's letter coming to the house on Sacramento Street a postcard came from Paul Moore.

5

In 1978, my mother died and I started to rely upon Bishop Moore for counseling and advice as he seemed to genuinely care about me and my psychological wellbeing. I set to work, finishing my college degree at the City University of New York (CUNY). I got my bachelor's degree in 1986, nearly ten years after I had started at Columbia University. My father died in 1983, and my mental status went into a deep tailspin.

Freud says that the death of a man's father is the deepest psychic pain a man can experience. Suddenly, in 1983, I learned I had friends I didn't know I had. There was a young lawyer who knew Bishop Moore and she knew Alan Roskoff, whom I knew from the many attempts to pass a gay rights bill in the New York City Council. Martha knew Alan's therapist Carol Cushman, and set me up with going to see the latter on the Upper East Side twice a week. I was a mess and stayed in therapy for about two or three years. I looked for work and settled at the first chance I got to work when the Immigration and Naturalization Service offered me a clerk position. Ronald Reagan was the President and it was December of 1986, and I felt maybe I could provide for myself. But the magic of letters in my life was to take a new incarnation. I started writing fairly frequently to Bishop Moore, and he would dutifully write and answer each of my letters. He was helping me pay for therapy with Carol Cushman. Through his discretionary fund as a bishop, he was providing $200 a month toward my therapy. We had built up an extraordinary correspondence. At one time Bishop Moore said he didn't think he had ever written as many letters to one person as he wrote to me.

I was living in a basement apartment, one block away from the house where I grew up with my mother and father and brothers and sisters and family. The job at the Immigration Service gave way to a job as a teacher in a Catholic school in Brooklyn. Since I had gotten my BA in 1986 and my MA in English Literature in 1988, I was able to start as a teacher at the Catholic school. The school was a very small Polish Catholic School. It was called Our Lady of Czestochowa. The Pope at the time was Saint Pope John Paul II, who was the first Polish Pope. Many but not all of the students at Our Lady of Czestochowa were Polish. The house where I was renting the basement apartment was owned by an elderly Polish couple John and Caroline Gielarowski. They took me in as a boarder to earn extra money. I had a hot plate and a warm bed. I'll never forget that the first night spent in that tiny apartment; I felt entirely safe and secure. Prior to finding that little apartment, I had actually spent a night in a homeless shelter. But here I was teaching in a Polish school and living in a Polish home. I continued to see Carol Cushman.

It was indeed a strange relationship I had with my analyst. She was new to her career. We would have our session twice a week, and I would be the last session, and then we would have another "real session"—we would walk around the block with her dog and catch up on life. I did this for two or three years. I felt Carol was becoming like a mother to me. She knew I wanted to write and teach and told me to always remember that Freud was a good writer. When I graduated from CUNY with my BA, Carol bought me a college ring. We really had a close relationship. Carol wanted me to be received into the "church," meaning the Episcopal Church. Though Carol was Jewish and from Philadelphia, she sat for three hours every Good Friday at the Episcopal Church on 5th Avenue. She would tell me privately that "Jesus was a tremendous healer too."

6

At some point, I wanted to see a gay therapist. I looked around and received two separate recommendations for an Episcopal priest and analyst Rev Edmond Hawley. Fr. Hawley was exactly the therapist I was looking for. There were no initial games or tension. He told me that he would see me but that his bishop—Bishop Paul Moore would have to send the money directly to me, and then I would pay him and would have to add whatever I could afford to the fee. I agreed to add $5 per session. Father Hawley was gay, but I felt safe with him. He told me many things about analysis. I think he wanted me to become an analyst. He said that there could not be any gifts between him and me such as Carol had done when she purchased the college ring. Because I was also seeing a psychiatrist and taking medication, he did not let me use "the couch." He said I could regress. He loved that I taught at Our Lady of Czestochowa School and advised me to stay in Catholic schools and to avoid public schools completely. He was familiar with the icon of Our Lady of Czestochowa. Coincidentally, at about this time there was put an icon of Our Lady of Czestochowa at The Cathedral of Saint John the Divine. The principal of the school was Sr. Redempta Kowalska, CSFN, and she said privately when we were talking in the teacher's lounge that they have to be sure about Episcopalians because the Polish National Church was in Communion with the Episcopal Church. At Our Lady of Czestochowa, my classes were small in comparison to those in public school or other Catholic schools. I taught there for three years, and one year my class had a total of twelve students. It was indeed like a private school education. The students were Polish, African American, or Hispanic, and some were Irish and Italian. I would love to ring the bell during recess in the yard. Each morning I would come to work in shirt and tie and jacket. As I walked down 25th Street in Brooklyn, I could see the Statue of Liberty.. There was extraordinary happiness in the Polish Community. Lech Wałęsa and the Solidarity Movement were strong in Poland. I would come in sometimes on a Monday morning and there would be new students from Poland. The Polish students were well ahead of the American students in Math and Science. They told me this was so because their schools in Poland were run by the Russians. But the Polish students did not like the Russians. The school had a music program and I had to teach my own gym class. My beginning salary was $15,000 a year and the school was always on the brink of a financial disaster. In the summers, I worked for the National Park Service at The Statue of Liberty as a Park Ranger. I took my classes to The Statue of Liberty and we played football on the grass. Though my analyst told me to avoid public schools, I was looking to go into public high school and was pursuing my license with the New York City Board of Education. I wondered aloud to myself: What if I wanted to have a family? How could I support myself, a wife, and children on $15,000 a year? I continued to see Bishop Moore and he would come to see me in my basement apartment in Brooklyn. He would drive his Mercedes and we would go for a ride. I talked to my analyst about the sex with Bishop Moore but was so happy with the therapy I was receiving I made nothing of it. I had a girlfriend at the time, a Greek American girl I had known since my Columbia days. I have always loved Greece and all things Greek. In fact, before I started my teaching career at Our Lady of Czestochowa, I went on a two-week vacation to Greece. I loved it. I particularly enjoyed seeing the traditional Greek dances, where men dance with men. I also continued my correspondence with Allen Ginsberg. It took a mystic turn when I realized that Allen Ginsberg was writing to me from his Post Office Box of "582" Stuyvesant Station to my basement apartment, whose address was "582"-81 Street Brooklyn. In one of my letters to Allen Ginsberg I told him of this coincidence and he wrote back these words: "Synchronicity is synchronicity, chance is chance, world is sacred so get yourself grounded and don't be so allusive, mysterious etc., etc. etc., speak plainly." As ever Allen Ginsberg

7

My friend and lover Gerald, who lived in San Francisco, had introduced me to numerology while we both studied at Columbia. And I had always been alert to numbers as I had been born on 5/4/54 and my address when I was born was **547**-80 Street. Another strange thing happened to me when I moved into the basement apartment with the address of 582-81 Street. I had taken with me some college books, which were in my parents' home, including an English literature compendium that had apparently belonged to my uncle George, who was the only college graduate in the house. He had graduated from St. Francis College in Brooklyn. One day while looking through the books I had moved to my new basement apartment, I noted that handwritten in pencil was the address 582-81 Street in the leaf of the English book. Had Uncle George lived—or purchased this book from someone who lived—in the building where I was now living in the basement? I agreed with Allen Ginsberg, synchronicity is synchronicity and chance is chance, but this was slightly eerie.

Both Carol Cushman and Rev. Edmond Hawley had graduated from the National Psychological Association for Psychoanalysis (NPAP). This is basically associated with the Theodore Reik Clinic, in New York, which was founded after the War to be a center of lay analysis. Freud himself was in favor of lay analysis. Through the years and through reading the books of Theodore Reik, I have come to appreciate more and more the work of this analyst who departed from Freud over everything being sexual. Reik felt that love was a motivation just as well as sex. I know I am not explaining this as well as I should, but in my life I have come to agree with Reik about love being equally as powerful a force as sex.

Currently, since 2006, I have been in therapy with a third analyst, Robyn Kopet, from NPAP (the Theodore Reik Clinic) and we work mostly on staying "grounded" as Allen Ginsberg recommended I do. And many times I talk about both Carol Cushman and Rev. Edmond Hawley in my sessions with my new therapist. This therapeutic relationship has lasted longer than any other. I saw Ed Hawley for about two or three years and then he said he was retiring and giving up his practice. I was very upset. So, Ed accommodated me somewhat. He saw me for sessions for a while at his house in Connecticut. He would meet me at the station and drive me to his home and then he would make a light lunch and say grace. We would sit looking upon the beauty of nature out the back of his house. Then he would drive me back to the station. Ed had AIDS and was in his eighties. One day after our session, he said he wanted to show me where he would be buried. So we got in the car and we drove to the cemetery, and he showed his grave. It had the stone on the grave and it said: "Edmond Hawley—priest and analyst"

My current therapist thought this was very strange to show me his grave, but I did not. I thought perhaps he wanted me to visit again someday when he was gone. Another strange thing was that in our last session, Fr. Hawley gave me a small statue of the Blessed Mother carved from coal that he said came from West Virginia, and he said he wanted me to have it. A few years later, it broke and I lost it, but I wondered about Fr. Hawley being so upset about Carol Cushman buying me a college ring that he too gave me a gift. The current therapist said from the outset: "No gifts!"

I continued seeing Bishop Paul Moore, and when his wife Brenda died, he wanted to see me more and more often. In 2002, we traveled to Patmos, Greece, together, and then in 2003 he passed away.

8

His daughter Honor Moore wrote a book *The Bishop's Daughter* about her father and used a false name for me and the relationship I had with Bishop Moore. As we were seeing each other more often near the end of his life, I was becoming more interested in establishing a relationship with a woman. I told him that I was "not going that way" when he insisted we go to bed. I met my wife Providencia Castro shortly before that trip to Greece in July 2002. Provi and I met for the first time on May 8, 2002, and it was as they say Love at "Primera Vista" Love at first sight. I was taken with the incredible physical beauty of Provi. Honor Moore told me when she was writing her book that her father complained after the trip to Greece that all I did was talk about my girlfriend. Provi is from Puerto Rico. She was a nurse for forty years and is a cancer survivor. She wanted me to read the Brazilian spiritual author Paulo Coelho and I did. We were taken with the words of Paulo Coelho that when two people fall in love the entire universe conspires. We were married in San Lorenzo, Puerto Rico, in 2004, at a mass attended by some of my Irish cousins who had flown to Puerto Rico for the wedding and several of my friends and my older sister Clare. The best man was my college roommate, Tim. It was an extraordinarily beautiful Saturday in San Lorenzo. I was working at the time with autistic children. I mentioned earlier that I had put myself through a School Psychology graduate program at Brooklyn College and I had a friend who had an agency that did applied behavior analysis with autistic children. It was exhausting work. And unlike the work I did with my own therapy was behavioral therapy. The School Psychology program I did at Brooklyn College was unlike most School Psychology programs, in that it was psychodynamic in its orientation. It was based on interpersonal theory. Thanks to Harry Stack Sullivan and the work he did with schizophrenics. My wife was a gift from God. To this day I swear I heard as clear as could be on the altar as we said our vows in San Lorenzo, Puerto Rico, the following beautiful and inspiring words: "God Loves Man and Miracles Happen" The miracle truly was meeting and marrying Provi. Provi made plans that with my educational credentials and her business savvy we could start a preschool nursery in Puerto Rico. With lots of work and getting many permits and licenses, we changed the first floor of Provi's house in Levittown, Puerto Rico, into a preschool/nursery. It was called Alegria Infantil and it was beautiful. I proceeded to get my psychology license in Puerto Rico, and on Saturday in addition to the preschool, I had a small practice for ABA therapy with children who were diagnosed with autism. Surely, miracles began happening in my life. Whereas before I had been a teacher in Catholic school and then in public high school, now I was the owner of a school. Provi and I were responsible for hiring teachers, for the training of the teachers, and for the collection of the tuition. It was our school! Provi called upon the expertise of a friend Profesora Angelita Cordero, who guided us through the intricacies of having a preschool. Ours was not just a nursery but a licensed preschool. We gained our license from the Department of Education in Puerto Rico. We had our certificates from the Department of the Family, and I continued with my psychology practice on weekends. Surely God had provided a miracle for Provi and me. I began to think and to pray to the icon of Our Lady of Czestochowa. Though I am not Polish, I felt the Blessed Mother had guided me to Provi, and the miracles were inevitable because we were such a good team. There were many friends in Puerto Rico. Many good times and enchanted places to see. But I was commuting between New York and Puerto Rico every two weeks. I was the English teacher at the preschool, and Provi just could not do it all alone. After seven years, it became hard to keep up the commute. We decided to close the preschool. I got a job in New York City with the express intention of retiring in Puerto Rico. We had married in 2004 when I was fifty years old and Provi was fifty-seven. Retirement was always just around the corner.

Michael and Providencia Gilbride – wedding San Lorenzo.
Puerto Rico. July 17, 2004

9

To go back, in 1990, Our Lady of Czestochowa closed and I was lucky to find work as a public school high school teacher. I had just recently gotten my license from the then New York City Board of Education. I was appointed to Samuel J. Tilden High School in East Flatbush as a Communications Arts teacher. The school population was almost entirely made up of Black Caribbean Island students. My department chairman was Mr. Joel Dick. Mr. Dick had been an English teacher at Tilden High School since the 1950s, when the student population was almost entirely Jewish. Mr. Dick became friends and partners and lovers with Mr. Everett Kerner, who also taught in the English Department at Tilden High School. In time, Mr. Kerner became the principal of the high school and his lover Mr. Dick became the chairman of the English department. That's the way it was when I joined the faculty in 1990. But, I was initially unaware of the relationship between Mr. Dick and Mr. Kerner. I found Mr. Kerner, the principal, to be an affable and professional man who was deeply concerned about reading. Mr. Dick was a perfectionist. Eventually the students themselves told me about the relationship between Mr. Dick and Mr. Kerner. Mr. Dick had an assistant whose name was Mr. John Devine. In 1990, I was very happy to be an English teacher at last. My professional ratings were all satisfactory. But I just could not get over the difference between a large public high school and the very small Catholic school (Our Lady of Czestochowa) that I had just left after three years. First, the behavior of some students was incredible. The halls of Samuel Tilden High School were another thing completely. There were gangs and fights, and at times even young teachers were known to join in the fisticuffs. I never did. But the fire alarm bell rang constantly throughout the entire school year because the teachers had lost control of the halls, and the students gained control of the fire alarm bell. Even while attempting to teach, there was the constant fire alarm bell. There was no way the teachers and administrators could regain control of the halls and, indeed, the school. I have a brother who is a year younger than me and he is quite conservative. When I told him stories of Samuel Tilden High School he would say to me: "You are making this up!" First, he thought it was just my fantasy that the chairman of an English department could be called Mr. Dick. I assured him my chairman was very professional and, in fact, that was his actual name. Later, I had to go to 65 Court Street for something and speak to one of the top administrators of the Board of Education. He said to me: "You would think he would change his name because of what students might say!" Then, when I told my brother his assistant's name was Mr. John Devine, my brother, who knew of my friendship with Bishop Moore and his Cathedral (St. John the Divine), thought I was lapsing into complete fantasy. My brother queried me further: "What do the students do? Dance on the desks?" In honesty, I said yes I had seen some students do just that. 1990 and 1991 were ideal years for me as a teacher. Students approached me in the halls as: "Sir." I was confused at first and then they explained that in the British Islands that is the appropriate way to call a teacher. I learned other British expressions such as a period is known as a "full stop." But all in all, many of the students were wonderful and wanted deeply to learn.

In some ways, I feel haunted by the summer of 1991. In June 1991, I successfully completed my first year as a high school English teacher at Samuel J. Tilden High School in Brooklyn. My department chair, Mr. Joel Dick, gave me an "S" rating for the year. I was made aware that my fellow teacher who

10

had started the same year as me, Marty, had received a "Doubtful" rating. Marty told me that Mr. Dick had written in his yearly rating that Marty had "balletic" movements. I encouraged Marty to file a case with the New York City Human Rights Commission, as a friend of mine, Andy Humm, had just been appointed a commissioner by the newly elected Mayor David Dinkins.

During the summer, I traveled to France—specifically Paris—for the first time in my life. In Paris, I fell in love with the French kids singing Elvis Presley at night. I wandered Les Halles, visited Pere la Chaise Cemetery, Montmartre, and the Sorbonne. I walked everywhere and went to see The Impressionists and The Rodin Museum. At Sacre-Coeur, I was deeply touched and carried home a card that read:

"Il y a ici Quelqu'un qui vous connait et qui vous aime"

(Here there is someone who knows and loves you)

For much of my life to that point, I had been involved in one way or another with the struggle for gay rights, specifically the passage of legislation in my home city of New York that protected the human rights of lesbian and gay people.

In 1991, I felt this had begun to actually become what it truly was, namely, a human rights struggle. I thought I would like to write one day of my own struggles and awareness. I wrote stories and sent them to the writer Howard Fast. David Dinkins marched in the Saint Patrick's Day parade with openly gay people for the first and the only time before it was taken to the United States Supreme Court. Though David Rothenberg had been a human rights commissioner, and though when my father died in 1983, I knew Professor Jim Levin and had him represent me because he had been an openly gay human rights commissioner for the City of New York, I, as a person, did not feel more challenged by the New York City Board of Education then I did in 1991. Marty and I both were new teachers working under extremely trying conditions. Samuel J. Tilden High School was run by the Principal Everett Kerner, who was amiable and seemingly well-liked. It was some time before I realized that the department chair, Mr. Joel Dick, was his partner and lover. Apparently, they had both been teachers in the English Department since the 1950s. Mr. Kerner became the Principal and Mr. Dick became the chairman of the English Department.

I myself had previously been a seventh-grade Language Arts teacher at a very small Polish/Catholic school. The Pope at the time was Polish and would later become Saint Pope John Paul II.

I survived two years at the Catholic school with a strict, very old-fashioned Polish nun as the principal. Then in my third year as a teacher, the nuns left the school and a new male principal was

11

brought in by the Department of Education for the Diocese of Brooklyn. I enjoyed a very good rapport with the new principal of this small Polish Catholic school and even had dinner with the principal. He was extremely cordial and outgoing. He confided to me that he lived with his male lover in Brooklyn. They were gay. He even introduced me to his lover.

I told him I had pretty much been in the process of leaving the Catholic Church over the gay issue. I had known many gay priests and many had "come on" to me and gone further. But to me the Church was very hypocritical as far as I could determine, about being gay.

I joined the Episcopal Church and was very active in my local Episcopalian parish. I was in psychoanalytic therapy with an Episcopal priest who was a psychoanalyst. My analyst's name was Rev. Edmond Hawley "Ed". Ed, though he was gay, felt I was making a tremendous mistake leaving the Catholic school system and going into the New York City public school system. When my own father died in 1983, I was encouraged by a friend, who was a female Episcopal priest and had been a lawyer working with Louis Nizer. She had decided to become a priest when her brother, John Henry, had contracted AIDS. She took care of her brother in San Francisco before he died. I saw another analyst at that time who was trained at Theodore Reik Clinic, just as Ed Hawley had been. At that time, I saw Carol Cushman twice a week for about two years. Carol had treated Allen Roskoff, who was active with me in the struggle to pass the New York City Gay Rights Bill. But I felt I needed an analyst who was himself gay. So, I started to see Ed Hawley.

I continued seeing Ed through my first year at Tilden High School. It was an eye-opening experience.

During the year, Iraq invaded Kuwait and the Gulf War began: the students protested and broke the window of the library door. Mr. Kerner took to the "PA" system and said the correct response to the start of war was prayer. I always admired him for that simple statement.

The night before the Gulf War actually started, Marty, the teacher who started with me at Tilden High School, and I went to a dinner/lecture at the Columbia Club in New York City, where I was at the time a member. The impending outbreak of war was discussed by Professor James Shenton.

I had always admired my own sense of quality as a teacher. I did not care to be in the classroom, which to me was a sort of "sacred space" without dealing with my own issues, in therapy. A month before I actually started my career as a teacher, I made a personal trip to Greece. I traveled to

12

Delphi, Corinth, Mykonos. I actually got a dream of being a "homeless" person in Greece—a strange dream.

During the summer of 1991, I worked from June to August as a National Park Service ranger at Castle Clinton in Battery Park, New York. As I mentioned, I wrote and sent my writings to Howard Fast about sexual awakenings while reading his book *April Morning* in 1968, when Robert F. Kennedy (RFK) was assassinated. I had become particularly aware of gay sexual feelings at the age of fourteen, in 1968, while on an altar boy outing to Bear Mountain, New York—the day RFK was shot and as he lingered the second day. I remember reading *April Morning* about the American Revolution and how it mentioned the Anglican Church.

That summer, the summer of 1991, in Crown Heights in Brooklyn, not too far from Samuel Tilden High School, a disturbance broke out after a procession when an Hasidic rabbi killed a local African American child and the long, simmering differences between the Hasidic community and the Black community exploded that summer. Tilden High School's students were almost entirely black students from the Caribbean. Given the explosion of tensions in September 1991, the New York City Human Rights Commission sent field teams to our local high school, simply to ensure the issue of "human rights" was treated sensitively. That summer after working for the National Park Service, I journeyed to Paris for the first time. The Sunday evening I returned to Bay Ridge, Brooklyn, an entire home on 86 Street in Bay Ridge exploded. The cause was a gas explosion. The neighborhood was increasingly Arabic.

While I was in Paris, I listened to the Friday call of the minaret and saw a mosque. I felt so intensely alive to the sensitivities of art and culture in Paris. I visited an amphitheater that was built by the ancient Romans. I read about the many who died before the Sacre-Coeur was built,

In September 1991, I was surprised to learn Mr. Dick and Mr. Kerner, my principal and department chair, were retiring. As I already stated, my fellow teacher Marty had filed a discrimination case with the New York City Human Rights Commission, based on "the perception that he was gay." I have to state that whether Marty was actually gay or not I never really knew. He told me he had a male friend that he held hands with. But he never told me any more than that. He told me he had taught in Israel for seven years. I knew Marty was from Brooklyn and seemed just like an "average guy."

But it was my belief, either right or wrong, that the sensitivity over the issue of being gay or straight was really not as much an issue, at least as far as New York City was concerned. And the employer of both Marty and myself was the New York City Board of Education.

13

In 1972, I started as a student at Columbia College. I had a lover, Gerald, whose father said "Kaddish" for him when he found out he was gay. He also told Gerald that the reason Gerald's mother had died of cancer was because Gerald was gay. One of the most pressing issues in 1972–1973 at Columbia was between the University President Bill McGill and the then Dean of Columbia College over the gay lounge which was funded by the alumni. Bill McGill was against a gay lounge and Dean Peter Pouncey was in favor. Both were ostensible Catholics.

Gerald and I became lovers, as I said. Gerald left after the first year and went to Berkeley in California after his father threw him out. Gerald graduated from Berkeley with a degree in History. I also dropped out of Columbia. I took courses at Staten Island Community College and at Brooklyn College. Unlike Gerald, my parents did not throw me out. I saw a therapist near Union Square in Manhattan with the help of a parish priest who knew some of my struggles. My parents were very active in our local Catholic parish. I too had been extremely involved. I had been a sacristan and worked in the rectory and then got myself elected to the parish council as a youth-delegate. I continued to attend parish council meetings even though I was a student at Columbia College.

In 1974–1975, I was re-admitted to Columbia College by Dean Henry Coleman on the condition I see the psychiatrist at St. Luke's Hospital. I did this and kept my appointments. But I also became active with some of the Jesuits who started a gay Catholic group. I even had a "gay" mass in my apartment on 110th Street. But I wished and hoped that somehow it could be resolved that one could be both gay and Catholic. I had told my parents, at about the age of eighteen, in a psychotherapy session with the therapist near Union Square, that I was gay. The therapist I remember was initially against my telling that to my parents. I remember my mother was shocked and seemed to blame herself. Where did she go wrong? My father, on the other hand, took it in stride and simply said: "You're making a mistake." But never did my parents disown me or throw me out of the house.

In 1974–1975, in April, I quit Columbia College for the second time. The psychiatrist at St Luke's, Dr. David Etess, said I was not "crazy." He described himself to me as the "son of a kosher butcher." He was convinced I could make it at Columbia College. He told me that it was his opinion that the "crux" of my issues was resolving the issue of being gay with the Catholic Church. He told me that I had to work out my "issues" with "them." To me that seemed daunting, to say the least. My college roommate and I had had sex with the same Catholic priest. Admittedly, we were both young and underage. But no one would believe, let alone help, someone who said they had had sex with a priest. I remember this same priest coming to my home in Brooklyn to take me on a "weekend" to Cambridge, Massachusetts, to see Harvard. I kept wondering really to the point of exhaustion (though it was the 1970s) why he couldn't leave the priesthood and live like a gay man, as my lover Gerald and I had already done. At least it would be more honest.

While I got to know the Jesuits at Columbia University, I came to hear from others of complete sexual exploitation of male students by Jesuit priests as being completely common. Just as usual, not

14

talked about openly. One of my roommates, a female friend, who was "gay-friendly" had heard so much of gay priests it became almost a joke, and she would say if priests can't have sex then: "Why don't they cut it off?" meaning their penis. Impossible to explain to someone outside the church that you still had some faith, though this was widely known.

I remember that at about the age of fifteen, I too wrote a letter to the Catholic Bishop of Brooklyn Francis Mugavero, and told him the priest in question was having sex with me and my friend Tim. Suddenly, though no response came to my letter, I remember the priest being moved to another parish and then another. Bishop Mugavero wrote a pastoral letter on how masturbation was still a sin. I kept a copy of the pastoral letter and wondered.

As I said, I worked in the rectory of our Catholic Church. As it was the 1970s, I had long hair. Bishop Mugavero made a pastoral visit to the parish, and I remember him stroking my long hair and saying "nice girl." All this while I was writing letters telling him the priest was having sex with the boys. I wonder now, how I could have explained my feelings, my mixed feelings, to my devoutly Catholic parents. And then the psychiatrist at St. Luke's telling me my problem was to work out being gay with the Catholic Church. Impossible! I thought.

So, in spring semester of 1976, I took off to San Francisco to see and live with Gerald. Gerald lived with a roommate in Pacific Heights, San Francisco. He was doing well. He also saw a psychoanalyst on Nobb Hill. I too began to see the analyst and fell in love with the idea of being gay and not repressed. We read Herb Caen, *Tales of the City*. Harvey Milk was the "Mayor of Castro Street." I had a friend who played Frisbee with me, and we slept in a parachute in an apartment near Coit Tower, in North Beach.

Before I left New York, I had attempted to come to know the Beat poets. My whole reason for going to Columbia was that I wanted to write. I met Allen Ginsberg in New York and William Burroughs. My roommate took classes with Joel Oppenheimer at

City College. While I was in San Francisco, Peter Orlovsky told me over the phone to go to City Lights Books and tell them I was working with Allen Ginsberg and they would give me all his poetry books. I did that and they did give me his books. In San Francisco that summer, it was also the bicentennial of the City of San Francisco being founded by Sir Francis Drake as well as being the Bicentennial of the United States. Jerry Brown was the young governor of California and some called him "Governor moon beam" because he wanted California to have its own space agency. But the way they talked on the streets of San Francisco was that only Governor Brown could recover California from the losses it had suffered while Ronald Reagan was the governor.

I never in my whole life felt more free and less challenged as someone who was gay than I did in San Francisco, in the summer of 1976. Near the end of the summer, many friends had visited us from Columbia College and slept on our sofa and floor. We sprang Gerald's younger sister, Marla, from her summer camp in Toronto, where she was staying with her grandparents. We had her come and stay with us in San Francisco. After thrilling at the perfect scores of Nadia Komenicjz at the 1976 Olympics in

15

Toronto, and after discussing the Hibernia Bank robberies and the Symbionese Liberation Army and Patty Hearst, Gerald and his sister and I were finally left alone.

Gerald, in all his affirmations that gay was good and that we were lovers and all that the summer of 1976 had meant to us both, proposed marriage to me beneath the Campanile and near the eucalyptus trees on Berkeley Campus. I considered what Gerald was proposing. I resolved that I did not yet have my college degree. I felt I had a reasonable chance of completing my degree at Columbia University in the fall. I said that Gerald had his degree from Berkeley and if I were to relate as an equal to Gerald, I would want to get my degree as well. Gerald was furious. He cursed me to his younger sister as abandoning him.

I flew back to New York City and I thought I would just return to Columbia. Tim, my roommate and friend from youth (he was the person who slept with the same priest as I had), and Ellen were both in the same apartment on 110th Street. As I already stated, I had promised to see the psychiatrist at St. Luke's Hospital. When I went to see him, I was taken aback by what he said when I returned from California. He said: "You went to California and you took drugs and now you can't come back to Columbia." That was the very same psychiatrist who said my problem was working out being gay with the Catholic Church. I retorted that we didn't take drugs in California and that in fact Gerald and I and his sister were in therapy with the same analyst in San Francisco. I was astonished. I was outraged. I should have stayed in San Francisco. Maybe I should have said yes to Gerald's proposal of marriage. It seemed gay people in San Francisco had more secure rights than those in New York—even in the Ivy League. I asked my parents to speak to Dean Coleman. Though my parents did speak to him, it was all to no avail. I had broken some golden rule—flown to San Francisco, entertained gay marriage from a longtime friend and lover, and continued in analysis while in San Francisco. Then when the summer was over, I thought I could finish my Ivy League degree so we could possibly be equals.

I remember thinking hard to myself at this point in my life. I remember that though I was young, I truly felt Columbia College and the City of New York did not understand a person wanting to be free and not discriminated against as a gay man. It seemed somehow that was taken for granted in the city of San Francisco but yet far from reality in New York City. I remember, in a very serious and solemn mood, walking up the enormous steps of The Cathedral of Saint John the Divine near the Columbia campus. I had been intimate with the Bishop before going to San Francisco. Somehow, my dream was that like the characters in Howard Fast's novel *April Morning*, which I had read as Robert Kennedy lay dying, that maybe the Episcopal Church could understand the need for gay human rights—if it was indeed impossible to resolve with the Catholic Church, and then maybe the Episcopal Church would stand for basic human rights. In my memory, there is a scene of myself, sitting at Saint John the Divine and writing a letter to Gerald in San Francisco, telling him I wouldn't give up the dream and that I would stay in New York until gay rights were a reality and officially recognized in New York City as human rights.

I started with my friend the Episcopal Bishop of New York, Paul Moore. I had met him before I went to San Francisco. I explained my problems with Roman Catholic priests sleeping with boys and men and then just not being able to say that they were gay.

16

Paul Moore took some prodding, but I knew the coalition working for passage of the bill in New York City. Later, I would become a spokesperson for the coalition. I like to think that due to my own personal efforts, Paul said he would testify before the New York City Council. I testified myself before the same council. Another time, I remember reading for the Episcopal Diocese of New York their statement on the need for gay human rights. Paul had asked me to read the testimony for the Diocese of New York at the City Council hearings.

I received a letter from Supervisor Harvey Milk in response to a letter I had written to him. Harvey Milk wrote: "It will be a long, hard struggle; that must be fought and will be won." I remember noting when I received the letter it was dated for April 4, 1978. This was the same date Martin Luther King had been assassinated ten years earlier.

In a final stroke of irony, it was President Ronald Reagan's Justice Department that challenged the role of the "one man; one vote" policy of the New York City Council which resulted in the restructuring of the council, and this made possible the passage of the "Gay Rights Bill." Ronald Reagan was an unlikely hero of gay rights in the City of New York. He had opposed the Brigg's initiative that sought to forbid gay teachers in California.

Jimmy Carter, who said he was in favor of human rights, on Father's Day in the middle of the Anita Bryant debacle was quoted that he could not support gay rights. I had personally gone down to Dade County, Florida, to work for gay human rights and felt particularly let down that especially on Father's Day Jimmy Carter had let down the cause of gay human rights. I had known that Jimmy Carter won in 1976 only by carrying New York State and he only won New York State by the margin of votes he tallied up in Greenwich Village. Many of those votes that put Jimmy Carter "over the top" were gay people who trusted him on the issue of gay human rights.

Were the conversations I had with friends, some of whom were Jewish, true? They said that the liberals sound good and look good, but they are not our friends. My friends had told me to read Laura Z. Hobson's *Consenting Adult,* which she wrote about her gay son Christopher. When the crunch comes, the liberals are just not there.

I thought of the prisoners who wore pink triangles, denoting they were gay. I thought of the Jews who wanted to deny that gay people also perished in the Holocaust. I even thought of Reagan's friend Barry Goldwater who had a gay grandson and, though conservative, supported gay human rights. All the politics! Left/Right !!! ... and still no human rights.

In 1978, Harvey Milk himself had every legal right that could be possessed at the time, and still his life could be taken in a few minutes by someone who hated him for being gay.

Back to 1991, surely my teacher friend Marty after all this would receive some justice from all places the New York City Human Rights Commission. Well, as I already said, in 1992, there was a change in administration at Samuel J. Tilden High School. I had been friends, I thought, with most of the English department, at least in a professional sense. I was surprised then by the reaction of some of the teachers with whom I worked. I mentioned something at one point about Marty, who was still a member of the department. She said in a very disparaging voice: "Oh—is he your friend?" I couldn't believe it. It was like I was being condemned by the association. The new chairman of the department was

17

anything but gay friendly, though she took over for Mr. Dick, who had been the lover of the principal. The acting principal was also not gay friendly. I remember one day in 1992, saying to myself: "This is enough!" Not only was Marty being blackballed for having made a complaint; I too was being tarnished and discriminated against for supporting his right to complain. Meanwhile, the world itself had changed. The Berlin Wall had come down. Mr. Kerner and Mr. Dick, the gay lovers who kept separate apartments, were no longer running the school or the department. I remember suddenly the comments in the teacher's lounge that were never spoken aloud while they were there were now being spoken. "Oh, if they had been straight lovers, it wouldn't have been allowed. They would have been sent to separate schools!" The mood and energy of the school had changed dramatically and it was anything but supportive of a gay teacher's rights.

I left school one day and simply went to Rector Street, where the New York City Human Rights Commission had its offices. I filed a human rights complaint against the New York City Board of Education but not on the perception of being gay, but on the fact that I was gay and felt intimidated and discriminated against by the sudden change in the school, and because I had supported Marty with his complaint. I openly said in my complaint that I was gay. I told my friend Andy Humm, who was a commissioner for the Human Rights Commission, and he said it could well be a test case. He, Andy, would recuse himself. Somehow word got to the acting principal that I had filed a discrimination suit. She took me aside one day and said I had a right to a personal life but that I was never to use the word "gay" in my classroom, not even in the context of a lesson. I was stunned. What about free speech? What about Walt Whitman? What about Allen Ginsberg? What about Harvey Milk's letter to me? "It will be a long hard struggle that must be fought and will be won."

MICHAEL GILBRIDE

Well the surprise was that the Human Rights Commission found "probable cause" for both Marty and for me as well. My friend, Andy Humm, who was a commissioner on the Human Rights Commission, did recuse himself.

But then, politics intervened. Rudy Giuliani was elected Mayor of the City of New York and stated that he wanted to abolish the New York City Human Rights Commission. Then came the real surprise, the Human Rights Commission reversed itself and found "no probable cause" for either Marty or for me. Of course, it was a different set of commissioners appointed by Giuliani and not Dinkins. I was outraged that the Law Department of the City of New York had offered as one of its responses to the complaint of discrimination for being gay that the City of New York Law Department felt the gay rights law itself (which I had struggled for and for which many had struggled for) was "unconstitutional!"

In my own attempt to circumvent the legalese, I determined to apply for another license from the Board of Education to teach English. In this process, I had to go to the Board of Education in Brooklyn and be interviewed by an examiner about the "problem" with the first license. I remember arriving in the room and seeing a man who had to be in his nineties slumped asleep at a desk. I had to wake him up literally. When I reviewed the specifics, I remember him saying to me: "OK, you can have the license but stay away from all the gay rights stuff." I had left a small Catholic school where the principal was ousted for being gay to go to a very large public high school where the principal and department chair were gay lovers. My friend was discriminated against for the appearance of being gay and then I myself did not feel secure. The Human Rights Commission seemed to know what gay rights were only to

18

Offer an opinion that the law I had fought for as a young man was "Unconstitutional!" Would New York City ever get it right?

I started this piece with writing about letters I had received, and consequently began to write to Allen Ginsberg and Bishop Paul Moore among others. Some of these letters seemed to have a magical quality. But what is it about letters that is so charming and heart-warming. It is nothing less than the fact that they tell a story. Each one a particular writing in time of things close to our heart of thoughts and problems. But each tells a story. At Columbia, I was a member of a special class. I was a member of the Columbia College Class of 1976. At that time, almost all other Ivy League Schools were going co-ed. I lived in a co-ed dormitory at Columbia, but the class of 1976 at Columbia College was the smallest in the Ivy League, and it was also the last all-male class. I learned many things I never had thought of before. For example, I learned of the importance of the oral tradition in ancient cultures and that stories and histories were originally handed from generation to generation by oral tradition by storytellers. I myself in my own family had loved to stay home and go and visit my ninety-five-year-old grandmother, who would tell me stories of old Brooklyn, of the family, and I often felt blessed just to sit with her and listen. We would enjoy a cup of tea, which she would pour and then she would talk to me. My grandmother was often home alone all day waiting for my aunt to return from work. My aunt and my grandmother lived on the second floor. While my family, parents and six children, lived on the first floor. I felt my grandmother was often left alone and I would love to just go visit her. I was, I guess, what they called back then somewhat of a "home-boy." I was not particularly athletic like my brother and the other kids in the neighborhood. Sometimes, we would watch the educational television network Channel 13 and it would be just me and my aunt and my grandmother. As I said, at the beginning in the summer, Fr. Peter would often come from Ireland and stay in the little room where my great grandmother had stayed. My great grandmother lived to ninety-nine and was active until she fell and broke her hip. I remember Nana, as we called her, saying to my mother: "What about the boy?" at one time. I was just "the boy."

As Nana got on in years reaching ninety-nine, I remember her sitting in her chair in the living room of the second floor with a blanket over her and watching Sunday television. Ed Sullivan, *The Disney Hour*, and then one night watching the Beatles on *The Ed Sullivan Show*. They told Nana this is what the kids are doing now and it seemed everything changed with the coming of the Beatles. Of course there were other memories of the television set. The Cuban Missile Crisis and President Kennedy coming on television and saying there were nuclear missiles pointed at New York. We never knew if we would be annihilated or not. Then, the Kennedy assassination. The television, providing non-stop coverage. It seemed with the television, we had entered a modern world where things such as oral tradition mattered not at all.

My grandmother would tell me her father came from London and married her mother. Though they were both Catholics when word got back to the family in Ireland that she had married an

19

Englishman, they sent her brother to Brooklyn to bring my great grandmother home. She would not leave America. As I said she came as an indentured servant and worked each day for wealthy people to pay off her indenture. She had come to America on her own at the age of seventeen near the end of the 1800s. There were things in the family that just were never spoken of. My great grandmother's maiden name was Sheridan and she came from the part of Ireland where they said General Philip Henry Sheridan had come from: County Cavan. It was always rumored that we might be a distant relative of General Sheridan, the Republican general whom they wanted to run as a Catholic for president. The general of whom Lincoln had said: "I like the little Irishman; he can fight." General Sheridan was also a member of a famous class at West Point that included the Southern General Robert E. Lee and General George Armstrong Custis.

My grandmother, over cups of tea, would tell me that her father Edward Cooper, who came from London, was the first male nurse in the State of New York and that she remembered him making potions and cures and powders. She would tell me that among his patients was Henry Ward Beecher, whom he took care as he was dying. Henry Ward Beecher was perhaps the most famous Protestant preacher at the time and a very famous abolitionist. Near the end of his career, he became involved in a sexual relationship that became a scandal.

My grandmother was a devout Catholic but several times she would complain to me "They are trying to make this a Catholic country." She loved Protestant hymns (Especially "That Old Rugged Cross") she learned as a child in Brooklyn. As I mentioned, it was rumored we might be related to General Sheridan. On the family farm back in Ireland in County Cavan, there is a "fairy fort". Actually, it was built by the Irish people to defend against Vikings' attacks. It's called Sheridan's fort and it's really nothing much more than a mound of earth in the form of a fort. My grandmother went to Ireland in the 1970s and I have a picture of her entering "Sheridan's

Fort" much in the way they did back then, they had inscribed the back of the photo with the day and date. In the 1980s when Fr. Peter took me around Ireland, I too got to take a picture at Sheridan's Fort. Strangely, I noted that the day and date of my picture was the same day and date inscribed on the back of my grandmother's picture only twenty-two years later. It was as though we both passed through the family stonehenge at the same time. I often feel a bond of love and connection with my grandmother and it mostly revolves around storytelling. Well, back to Henry Ward Beecher, the Protestant preacher of the late 1800s, who was an abolitionist and then got involved in a sexual affair.

In meditation and reflection and reading, I began to think my relationship with Bishop Moore and the struggle for gay rights in New York City in the 1970s and 1980s might bear a relationship to Henry Ward Beecher. Bishop Moore was described as the most well-known Episcopal, if not Protestant, clergyman of his day. I had an affair with Bishop Moore that became known with the publication of his daughter's book *The Bishop's Daughter* by Honor Moore. It led to a fall from grace for Bishop Moore, even though he had passed away. Both Henry Ward Beecher and Paul Moore were "pushing the bounds of freedom" and both were prominent Protestant clergyman. What is it about the times we live in? It is as though the French saying "La plus ca change, c'est le plus meme chose" (the more things change the more they remain the same) is true and bears examination. As though things which were true about freedom and liberation and Protestant theology of the 1800s are then again in a strange way repeated

Statue of General Philip Henry Sheridan
by Gutzon Borglum 1908, Washington, D.C.

20

In the 1980s—as though time was just a concept we measure feebly. My grandmother and I both passed through Sheridan's Fort—or a family stonehenge captured on photos with the same date and day, only separated by years. Some of what my grandmother thought and felt and believed had been transmitted to me in stories, but essentially the conflicts and problems and hopes and dreams of both of us remain linked. It is as though the incident in 1976, when I went to San Francisco with the gold watch my grandmother had engraved and given me, and then lost and miraculously recovered from Joel Jaffer, spoke a timeless truth. Dreams come, dreams fade, dramas occur and go away; lives come and go, and yet we are bound to certain people to certain struggles basically forever. Our lives repeat in many ways the lives of those who have gone before us. What links us are stories and love. We try to measure time with clocks and watches and calendars but some things are timeless, the most important being love. The struggle I bore for gay rights in the 1970s in New York City in some ways was as important as the struggle for abolition. Both involved incredibly talented and important clergyman. Both questioned what rights we have as Americans. Both split families and both united people in struggle. But the church was there for both struggles. The church was deeply involved in both struggles.

When I think of someone telling me charming old and wonderful stories such as my grandmother, the only other person I think of in my life who could do that was Bishop Paul Moore, Jr. He would tell stories of the church of prayer of people being there of those who were never to be found. And the stories were right out of the old-fashioned classic world my grandmother belonged to with her stories. I used to love to hear Bishop Moore talk of the French worker priests and his stories of his making his first confession and how it changed his life. If Paul was gay, it gave me strength to know that I too could be like Paul and marry. Of course, I could not have eleven children. It is true that one day after more than thirty years of writing letters, getting together, sharing our conflicts hopes and dreams, I sat on the sofa of his house on Bank Street as he made drinks. He told me wonderful stories; stories of famous people, of simple people. He did take off his Bishop's ring and slipped it onto my finger and said: "Now you are the Bishop of New York." It was done playfully and in love and I did not take it seriously. But Honor Moore told me that many Episcopalians were aghast when that story with the ring became known. In his book, *Presences*, Bishop Moore says that one time in Jersey City when saying mass, there was no wine and somehow the wine was substituted with whiskey. Bishop Moore said he was sure Our Lord understood. I feel the same way about the bishop putting his ring on my finger.

In 2002, on a bus in Greece, I was with Bishop Moore. He was sitting next to me and after years of knowing each other, we had come to go to the Cave at Patmos. I could see he was psychically in pain. He had been prohibited from saying mass because of inappropriate sexual advances. They wanted him to go to Menninger's for treatment as a sexual abuser. He would not go, and his wife Brenda stood up for him with the Presiding Bishop. But Paul, in his eighties, sat next to me on the rough and dusty bus ride to the beach through the Greek landscape. He told me as we sat next to each other, in his mind he said over again the words to the mass as prayer. I knew I was deeply privileged to know Bishop Moore and regret any way in which I may have contributed to his suffering. Before he died, he used to talk to me many times about The Incarnation of Our Lord. To imagine that Our Lord Jesus became one of us and

21

Was with us. So many times, in Catholic school I had heard the term The Incarnation, but Bishop Moore, near the end of his life, was in wonder as a child would be at such an amazing concept. That somehow through all the stuff we go through—some of it so awful and some of it not important at all to think—that Jesus Christ became man and suffered on this earth for us to know God. It is an amazing concept. It is beyond our comprehension.

I think Bishop Moore and my grandmother were from the same old world where stories are the stuff of dreams, where we can live and hold onto the stuff that is told to us rather than what we see on the television or the internet, and where there really are amazing human beings. Both Bishop Moore and my grandmother were to me profoundly religious people. Both had extraordinary relationships with the Lord. And both somehow knew there had to be more than just the Catholic Church. In my life, I have returned to the Catholic Church. I know it full of truth and grace and wisdom. But then there are times when I think of my grandmother, the most devout Catholic woman I knew, rebelling at the thought that "they were trying to make this a Catholic country." And Bishop Moore, who told me many times he was catholic with a small "c", was Anglo-Catholic. But knowing Bishop Moore encompassed so much more about Jesus than just Catholicism. He was a friend, a lover, a teacher, a Christian.

April 1968. I was thirteen years old. I would be fourteen in May. I was scheduled to graduate from grammar school in June. I had chosen my Confirmation name: Paul. 1968 was an election year. I was rooting for Senator Robert Kennedy. Upstairs from our apartment on the first floor, my grandmother lived with my two aunts, Dorothy and Alice, and Dorothy's two teenage girls. Aunt Dorothy was very intelligent. She would take me aside at my graduation and say the only two members of this family to have received the "General Excellence Medal" were me and her. Aunt Dorothy had lost her husband Uncle George. He was the only member of the household to have graduated from college; Saint Francis College in Brooklyn. Aunt Dorothy was a widow with two teenage daughters. Aunt Alice had married and lost her only child and was separated from her husband. Aunt Dorothy had an important job. She worked as a secretary for the Board of Education. April of 1968, the public school teachers went on strike in New York City. Aunt Dorothy would come home each night, very worked out and tired, and talk about: "That Mr. Shanker." Al Shanker was the President of the United Federation of Teachers. John Lindsay was the Mayor of the City of New York and things were not going well. There had been a transit strike in 1966 and in February of 1968, the garbage men went on strike. The Vietnam War was raging. My father's family owned Todd Shipyards, which last made great profits during the Second World War, but now with Vietnam, profits were up again. To be clear, my father did not work at the shipyards. He was a humble truck driver. He was a teamster with six kids to feed. Given Senator Kennedy's prosecution of the teamsters when he was Attorney-General it was indeed funny that we were rooting for him to win the presidency. But my father was a Democrat and I liked them better than Nixon.

I too worked and had a job. I worked as the Sacristan at Saint Anselm Church. I had to wear a cassock and set up for masses on Sunday. When the lector didn't show up, I would fill in. Then I was asked to work in the rectory as well as continue as the sacristan. So I had two jobs at church. In the rectory, I answered phones and answered the door and wrote messages for the priests. There was a

22

Young deacon at Saint Anselm's. He was dynamic and he liked John Lindsay. His name was Deacon Petroski. He read Rod McKuen and other poetry; and he wrote as well. He was not yet a priest. I was in love with Joan Baez and was reading her book *Daybreak*, which Deacon Petroski had already read, and he recommended I read *Catch-22* by Joseph Heller about the Korean Conflict.

I was working at the rectory the night in April when Martin Luther King was assassinated. I remember I came home and my older sister was with her then boyfriend. No one was paying any particular attention to me and no one was paying attention to the transistor radio I had which was announcing the breaking news that Martin Luther King had been shot. I didn't quite know much about who Dr. King was, but I knew this was important and I knew it involved the church. There was an ecumenical service at Saint Anselm that I took part in memory of Dr. King. Deacon Petroski went off to complete his studies but had been very friendly to me and asked me to stay in touch.

Dr. King was shot on April 4. My Aunt Dorothy had a stroke and she passed away on April 28. I turned fourteen on May 4. I sat myself down and wrote a letter to Deacon Petroski and told him about the death in my family and asked for guidance as a Catholic. Deacon Petroski wrote me back and told me that if we believe in Jesus and love, we do not die. He asked to get together with me before his ordination. I was willing. It would be two more years before his ordination in May 1970. There were other letters. There were times we got together. We saw the movies *Woodstock* and *2001; A Space Odyssey*. I really liked Deacon Petroski.

To make a long story short, Deacon Petroski was after me sexually and I was unaware. He took me to look at colleges in Massachusetts, namely Harvard in Cambridge. There were shared hotel rooms, shared beds. I was taken advantage of by then Father Petroski. I had gone to Father Petroski's ordination mass. And there were memory cards distributed. I kept two of them. One was a quote by Dag

Hammarskjold: "We cannot choose the frame of our lives but what we put into it is ours." The second was a quote from Dr. Martin Luther King: "I can never be all I am meant to be until you are all you are meant to be." The quote from Dr. King spoke to me. Shortly, after Dr. King was assassinated, a deacon and would-be priest started writing beautiful letters to me about Christ, about death, and about life. In one of his letters, Deacon Petroski wrote me always and whatever cost always "Choose Life". Deacon and Father Petroski was speaking to my young soul. Later, much later in my life, I tried through the Reconciliation and Compensation Program with Bishop Nicholas DiMarzio of Brooklyn. I tried to once again to come to terms with what had happened with Deacon Petroski. First, I must say very clearly and very certainly, in no way do I wish harm to the soul of Deacon/Father Petroski. I completely, as much as another human being possibly can, forgive him. We had sex. He could not help me back then. But I believe that Fr. Petroski was a gay man. I think because of the priesthood he could not have sex and therefore was trapped in his career. Whether consciously or unconsciously, Father Petroski taught me an awful lot. I was abso-lutely a "babe in the woods" when it came to knowing about gay men, let alone priests having sex. I thought priests don't have sex. My feelings are still very much with Fr. Petroski. I don't think he was willfully trying to hurt me. His letters are still among my possessions, though I don't know if I can call them "magic" letters. Sadly, they make me think he, Fr. Petroski, suffered. I too

23

Suffered and was confused. Absolutely, I wrote a letter to then Bishop Francis Mugavero. Absolutely, Fr. Petroski was moved around. I later heard that Fr. Petroski died of AIDS. Very sad. I think that it was the church itself that could not be honest, and I do not blame Fr. Petroski. Later through the IRCP (Independent Reconciliation and Compensation Program) process, I spoke with Bishop James Massa, who said back then the church was dealing with Vietnam. But so was I and so was Fr. Petroski. Part of my family was making record profits on defense contracts. I was opposed to the Vietnam War and so was Father Petroski. The church was in bed with many people who were choosing death. Death for Vietnamese peasants, death for young American kids who died for their country in a war which it is now known the government knew all along they could not win.

Even now as I think of the letter written to me by Harvey Milk ten years to the date after Martin Luther King was assassinated, I think those words are true for gay people. "It will be a long hard struggle that must be fought and will be won." But I still think those words involve the card from Father Petroski's ordination. Father Petroski is gone now from this world, but in very real ways, sometimes he still lives for me as an inspiration for someone who would even risk his priesthood. The card from Martin Luther King says: "I cannot be all I was meant to be until you are all you were meant to be." Father Petroski is still with me at times in prayers; in thoughts of Vietnam and Columbia and thoughts of young people and the church. I still pray for Fr. Petroski. I still sometimes feel I will never be all I am meant to be unless I can make sense of those days and those things that happened back when. I was seeing a psychiatrist when I was approaching the Independent Reconciliation and Compensation program. He was an Episcopal priest and a psychiatrist. He was very correct. He asked that what you are supposed to do when you write a letter to the Bishop. You are a teenager and they start moving around the priest-offender. The Bishop ignores your letter and you are left to believe you are crazy and powerless. The priest and psychiatrist's name was

Dr. Jeffrey Hamblin. He told me they can never pay you enough money for what was taken from you as a youth. I tend to believe that. It started me on a mission in my own life to find truth. It led to me making an appointment and meeting Bishop Paul Moore. In my first meeting with Bishop Moore, he wrote back to me that you have to be careful about the truth. You always have to balance one good against another.

Just this year, I have come across a pastoral letter written by the now Episcopal Bishop of New York which says that Bishop Moore is now thought to be a "serial sexual predator." Paul Moore was so much more than that but I was attempting to come to terms with Roman Catholic priests who had sex with males and then couldn't come out as gays. Even Bishop Moore couldn't do it. But that doesn't diminish the respect and love I had for Bishop Moore. Very few people I have met, in fact I can't think of any, are without some fault, even minor faults. The only person who ever walked this earth and who was without fault was The Lord Jesus Christ and he was crucified.

My life has been dominated by a force other than Jesus. That is of Freud and psychoanalysis. I've been in therapy since I was eighteen. But I've always been intrigued and even "smitten" by Freud. In 1997, Allen Ginsberg died and I had an overwhelming feeling he returned to God. I had always most admired a quote I read from the "Gay Sunshine" interview of Allen Ginsberg. The story is that he is at the doors of Heaven and God says come in, but Peter, his lover, is not there. Allen says to God, "Then it cannot be Heaven if Peter is not there," and does not enter Paradise. I have the same feeling about people I have loved. If they are not there I guess it really won't be Heaven. One night at his house

24

On Bank Street, after a few drinks, Bishop Moore turned to me and said, "Well we are both going to hell anyway. But there will be far more interesting people there than in Heaven." In 1997, I was making plans with my friend Susana Namnum to go to Italy. We made plans to go to Rome and Florence and see all the art, and even made a side trip to Assisi. But that week Allen Ginsberg died; Susana's father also unexpectedly passed away. Susana's father was a Mexican-Lebanese psychiatrist/psychoanalyst. Susana told me that even though she was sad her father had died, she felt he would want her to continue the trip to Italy. So, we continued the trip. Susana's father had made a request that when we were in Rome we see Michelangelo's "Moses", as this was the only sculpture of Michelangelo that Freud had analyzed. In 1913, Freud had spent three weeks analyzing this sculpture of Moses that has horns. He felt Moses was in a particularly strange psychic state having just received the tablets and thinking he would smash them because the Israelites were worshipping the calf.

At Columbia in 19721973, I had spent an entire semester on William Shakespeare's *King Lear*, which was the only Shakespeare play Sigmund Freud had analyzed. He felt Lear could not come to terms with his impending death. But having been in therapy since 1972, I am always intrigued when I see an interpretation of a piece of art or writing that Freud himself analyzed. Susana and I arrived at the church where the "Moses" was "just in time." The church was empty except for us and we stood before the "Moses" for about half an hour before the church closed. Nowhere near the three weeks Freud spent in 1913. But, I felt we had honored Dr. Namnum's request to see the work of art analyzed by Freud.

I stay in therapy these days for two basic reasons. First, Allen Ginsberg told me I needed to be grounded. And I agree with that assessment. But the other reason I stay in therapy has to do with my previous analyst Rev. Ed Hawley. I had heard of people being in therapy for "insight," but when I was in therapy with Ed, I frequently received psychodynamic insight. He would often remind me of things I had read when reading

Freud, and open my mind to new insights. Not as frequently does that happen these days with my therapist Robyn. I believe it is for two reasons: first, her style is very different than that of Rev. Hawley, and second I am much older. That is not to say one can't think in new ways when one is older, but it happens less frequently.

I have in my bedroom a corner for prayers and meditation. It has many, many icons mostly of saints and holy people. At the center of my icons is a treasured icon that Paul Moore gave me when I graduated from my School Psychology program at Brooklyn College. It is of the Blessed Mother holding her child. On the left side is a representation of St. Michael the Archangel and on the right side is the Prophet Elias. I've had the icon blessed a few times. The first time I was with friends at a Greek Orthodox Cathedral in Manhattan and spoke with the priest. He said what I needed to do was have him place the icon in the holy of holies in the Greek Orthodox Cathedral where only the priest goes for 40 days and they would pray and bless this particular icon. I did that. But later, I wanted to also have it blessed by a Roman Catholic bishop. I was going to a Novena to the Sacred Heart at the Visitation Monastery in Bay Ridge and Bishop Nicholas DiMarzio was celebrating the mass. I took Paul's icon and

25

after mass asked Bishop DiMarzio to bless the icon. He did. Paul told me that the icon hung every working day of his life as bishop on the wall at the Cathedral of St. John the Divine in his office. He told me that in 1939, just before the outbreak of the Second World War, he was on a trip to Greece with his mother and made a trip to Mount Athos. He liked this icon because the Madonna had a nice smile. I've had the icon assessed as to how old it was by an iconographer and he said he would say it was definitely a Greek icon and was painted in about 1830.

After Bishop Moore died, I got together with his daughter Honor Moore and we shared letters Paul and I had written for her book *The Bishop's Daughter*. Honor gave me a wooden pectoral cross of Paul's. It is a Jerusalem cross. I wore the pectoral cross around my neck every Saturday night at Saint Francis of Assisi Church in Manhattan where I was an altar-server and a Eucharistic minister. After a while the iconographer I knew did a course at Saint Francis, and I asked if he would paint a personal icon of Bishop Moore for me. He said he would. He prayed and fasted and read Honor Moore's book, and I gave him the icon the Bishop had given me, and the pectoral cross. He painted the new icon, and in it Paul is handing me the pectoral cross. I learned a great deal from the course which was given on icons. I learned the word: "Prosopon." Prosopon is a Greek term that comes from the mask or face that actors in Greek theater wore to reveal a manifestation of their emotional state. Prosopon means the self-manifestation of an individual extending by means of other things. The "hypostatis" occurs when one sees in the face the representation the icon painter intended. I learned that the eyes of the icon are the most important part of it. As scripture states, "The eyes are the windows to the soul."

When Paul died, I was working with autistic children, and it is very well-known that one of the diagnostic procedures for diagnosing autism is to determine that the young child will not "look the other in the eyes." As I became practiced as a psychologist, I learned so much is revealed, or at least believed to be revealed, by the eyes. I was trained on the Rorschach, and know very well the first thing a Rorschach examiner says is: "Tell me what you see." Thus in a hope to reveal what is in the subconscious, the Rorschach examiner asks about sight.

Among my many icons in my prayer corner, are the original icon Bishop Moore gave me and looking at this icon is the one I had painted of Bishop Moore giving me his pectoral cross. Beneath the icon, I have a stone painted in Greece that says "Patmos." Each Saturday night after mass I faithfully place Paul's pectoral cross below his icon. I also have several icons of Our Lady and the Lord. I have the icon of Our Lady of Czestochowa (the black Madonna) that was said to have been painted by Saint Luke on a table that was in the Blessed Virgin's home. I also have Our Lady of Perpetual Help. I have icons of many, many Saints, Henri Nouwen and C.S. Lewis and even Harvey Milk.

Having asked Bishop DiMarzio to bless both the icon Bishop Moore gave me and the one I had painted of Bishop Moore, I feel I've made the journey back to the Catholic Church. I was part of the Independent Reconciliation and Compensation program at the Diocese of Brooklyn and received a settlement for what happened years ago with the priest/perpetrator. The Episcopal priest/psychiatrist

26

I consulted at the time assured me no amount of money can make up for what was taken from me as a youth. But I can't help but wonder at the school I taught at when I first became a teacher for the Diocese of Brooklyn. Had the church been open back then to what happened, the amount of money given to me perhaps could have saved that entire school from closing, and I could have kept my first job as a teacher and avoided all that happened in the public schools. But the fact is the church was not open back then to settling with victims of clergy sexual abuse. It made me think of the arrangement I had to come to with my other analyst who was an Episcopal priest with Bishop Moore. Fr. Ed Hawley was very straight about the way money went back then and said, "Bishop Moore must pay you and then you pay me."

I loved myself as a teacher at Our Lady of Czestochowa and go back each year to think of those days. Though I was in a relationship with an American Episcopal (Protestant) clergyman, the Pope was John Paul who was a Saint and was Polish. I loved the icon of Our Lady of Czestochowa and my analyst at the time knew it well. The Black Madonna. As I mentioned, my father's family had shipyards during the Second World War and up until the Vietnam War. All my father's brothers worked in the shipyards. When the Solidarity Movement began in Poland while Reagan was President and John Paul was Pope, in the Gdansk shipyards, I felt a special feeling of solidarity myself with the workers.

Of all the things I did with Bishop Moore, and then in coming to know Bishop DiMarzio, I have to say the very human act of sharing a meal meant the most. When I was a young child, I've mentioned that I had a great grandmother and she would offer to feed me when I visited her home around the corner. I would wonder and not feel right about eating her food as she was poor. But as I got to know Bishop Moore, he would cook and prepare meals for us both in his home. It is such an equalizer a human act. I felt Bishop DiMarzio, to his credit, did that exactly right having dinner with the victims of clergy sexual abuse. It is also something I learned as a student from ancient times. The ancients knew it as basic hospitality. In our modern and fast moving society the basic skills, such as hospitality and storytelling, are often breached to our detriment.

I feel I've grown up around a great deal of death since I was young. When I was a teenager, there was Vietnam and the many young men and women who gave their lives for a war, which has been revealed our country knew it could not win. And there was the scourge of drugs. Several of my friends as a teenager lost their lives to drugs. Then came the scourge of AIDS and the many young people lost to AIDS. Now we live in a time of pandemic and it is estimated by autumn, nearly 200,000 Americans will have died of COVID-19. It makes me reflect upon the words my priest/perpetrator wrote to me in one of his letters: "At whatever cost choose life."

In the past week I have prayed and made a virtual online novena to The Sacred Heart of Jesus. One of the readings was from a letter from Saint Paul. Of all my reflections upon letters, and this one by Saint Paul from the Second Letter to Timothy was the most meaningful:

"So you, my child, be strong in the grace that is in Christ Jesus. And what you heard from me through many witnesses, entrust to faithful people who will have the ability to teach others as well. Bear your share of hardship along with me like a good soldier of Christ Jesus. To satisfy the one who recruited

27

h im, a soldier does not become entangled in the business affairs of life. Similarly, an athlete cannot receive the winner's crown except by competing according to the rules. The hardworking farmer ought to have the first share of the crop. Reflect on what I am saying, for the Lord will give you understanding in everything.

Remember, Jesus Christ, raised from the dead, a descendant of David: such is my gospel. "for which I am suffering, even to the point of chains, like a criminal. But the word of God is not chained. Therefore, I bear with everything for the sake of those who are chosen, so that they too may obtain the salvation that is in Christ Jesus, together with eternal glory." This saying is trustworthy:

> If we have died with him,
>> we shall also live with him.
> If we persevere,
>> we shall also reign with him.
> But if we deny him,
>> he will deny us.
> If we are unfaithful,
>> he remains faithful,
>> for he cannot deny himself.

2 Timothy 2 (1-13)

My confirmation name was Paul, and since I was a teenager I've been fascinated by St. Paul. But I believe the last line of this letter from the Second Letter of St. Paul to Timothy is the most important to me. In a very easy way it says to me that Christ cannot lie. He cannot deny himself. When I was wondering about what had happened to me as a youth, I spoke to some who said what was broken was "basic trust" of Christ by a sexual predator. But I feel I cannot deny these experiences happened in my life. I cannot deny that perhaps the two most important Christian people in my life were Bishop Paul Moore and my grandmother. Now, some label Bishop Moore as a serial sexual predator but that denies all that he was as a human, as a Christian, as a Protestant clergyman. One of the most persuasive Catholic Bishops I have ever heard explain this said that Faith, Hope, Love—these are the most important virtues. But in the fulfillment of time, our faith will be rewarded and accounted for; our hope will be fulfilled and true and the only one that truly remains in the end when we are in the Kingdom with the Lord is Love. Love is the greatest. "Faith, Hope, Love" these three remain, but the greatest is Love." I have learned in time with work with a therapist, trained in Theodore Reik, about the transcendent power of Love. I have seen love which always existed in my family in the person of my grandmother come to fruition in the form of

28

Storytelling and hospitality. But who can say about Love. John the disciple said: "God is Love!" and to that I can only offer my simple "AMEN."

AFTERWARD

Just as I prepared Letters for publication; there appeared serendipitously at the same time an article in "The New York Times," by critic Dwight Garner: "Mourning the Letters That Will No Longer Be Written, and Remembering the Great Ones That Were." Garner mourns about how letters are disappearing and how during this pandemic he yearns for nothing as much as a good letter.

Despite my writing for publication my short book Letters; I had forgotten the many letters I had written as a young person. Garner's article caused me to remember writing when I was young a letter to Russell Baker at The New York Times about an article he had written during the Nixon impeachment. Russell Baker had made the case in his article in The Times that everything could be broken down to either Presidential or Congressional. I plead my case to Baker and asked: "Am I, a teenager in favor of impeachment, Presidential or Congressional. I typed the letter on my portable typewriter at the time. Baker's response was that he didn't have enough information but that my poor little portable typewriter was definitely Congressional

I wrote many letters as a young person because I believed the saying that:"the pen is mightier than the sword." Many of my letters were addressed to Mario Cuomo and Ed Koch about two issues important to me: gay rights and capital punishment. As an afterwards about my relationship with the human being I shared more letters than any other in my life: namely, Bishop Paul Moore I reflected upon some other salient points. Paul Moore once told me he had a conversation with Prince Charles during the royals visit to New York for the 1976 bicentennial. Charles asked Paul Moore where he stood on capital punishment. Paul told me he responded that he was against it; to which Prince Charles responded: "That's because you are a bishop."

Reflecting now, I think the conversation showed Paul Moore on the right side of Catholic Theology. Recently, Pope Francis has added capital punishment to the Catechism of the Catholic Church as a sin against life.

MICHAEL GILBRIDE

In 1995, I traveled to Greece on my own. I had booked a trip to one of my favorite places in the world but it did not include Patmos when I booked the trip. To this very day, something happened that I cannot explain. This trip was seven (7) years before I went with Bishop Moore. I arrived in Athens and checked into my hotel and slept until I could get a cab to Piraeus to board my cruise the next day. Somehow, when I got to the port of Piraeus, I was put on another cruise ship not the one I had booked. (This was before the terrorist attacks of 9/11). The cruise ship I was put on was a much better ship and the room I was given was a much nicer room with a much better view. After the ship departed, I found out the next to last destination of this cruise was Patmos. The last destination of the trip was to Istanbul. From the ship I phoned my travel agent in New York to ask what to do. After several worried conversations, I was told it would be alright and the agent would fly me back free of charge first class from Turkey on Austrian Airlines. I finished the cruise with my very first visit to the island of Patmos and then went to Turkey.

So, I had a better ship, a nicer room, a better tour and would see Patmos after all and would be flown home first class on Austrian Airlines. Yet, I couldn't explain how this fortuitous accident had occurred. To top everything off, when I got back to New York my travel agent returned all my money because I had insurance and the trip was not the one I had booked. Was this accident only "serendipity?" It occurred as I said about

Seven (7) years before my second trip to Patmos with Bishop Moore. My thoughts were only in one direction and I still believe that it was God calling me to Patmos before I went there with Bishop Moore.

Later I explained to Paul that I had an overwhelming experience of John the Apostle; (John the Divine) on the island of Patmos. It was indeed the reason Paul and I chose to go to Patmos in 2002. On the trip with Paul though, the bishop was reading "The Book of Revelation" and neither one of us had a mystical or magical experience. Paul's reaction was the correct one: "You can't make spiritual experiences happen. We had discussed going to Fatima, Portugal instead of Patmos but because off my unexplained experience in 1995 we chose the island of Patmos.

Paul often told people of a spiritual experience he had in Jerusalem at the Church of the Holy Sepulcher. He said when he first visited the Holy Sepulcher he felt a weight on his shoulders telling him to kneel down.

I had just met my future wife before the trip I took to Patmos with Paul.

In 2002, after I had met and was living with Providencia, my wife, I found out Paul was diagnosed with cancer. My wife Provi and I visited Paul at his Bank Street home. Paul said he wished he could be at our upcoming wedding but he would be there in spirit he promised. We were married in July 2004 and Paul passed away in May of 2003. My wife initially said I had to stop all contact with Paul when she found out I had gone to Patmos with Paul in 2002. But when she found out he had cancer she was just incredible. Stupendous!

She told me that she had learned in her own overcoming of cancer that friends have to rally around you and support you. Provi my wife asked me if she who had been a nurse for more than forty (40) years and had overcome cancer could take care of Paul. I knew Paul's family was taking care of him. I discouraged Provi and may have been wrong. I called Paul's home the day before he died and they told me he was sleeping a great deal. I spoke briefly with one of Paul's sons and to one of his daughters.

On May 1st, 2003, the icon Paul had given to me which he said he had purchased on a trip in 1939 to Greece with his mother shortly before the outbreak of the Second World War and which he said had hung on his wall every day of his working life; fell mysteriously off the wall of my apartment. The day was May 1st which that year was Greek Orthodox First Friday and in the Catholic World the Feast of Saint Joseph the Worker. When the icon fell on the floor, I knew Paul had passed. Some might say of the icon falling off the wall that: "accidents happen." But like the "accident" of my first trip to the island of Patmos where all that I wanted was given I could not just call it an accident. I could not call it just an accident when I got a free trip to Patmos and I could not call it just an accident that the icon Paul had given me fell from the wall on the day he died. It was Greek Orthodox Good Friday. Does not God sometimes work through accidents? There are those who go so far as to say there are no accidents.

There was something I tried to relate to Honor Moore about what did happen on our trip to Greece in 2002. There was a scheduling error with the ships and we had to spend the night on the island of Samos. This had not been planned. Something about that single night on Samos was tremendous to my relationship with Paul Moore. He was wearing a black shirt and we had time freed up from no where. We were able to eat fish. I truly sensed Paul that night not as bishop but as priest. He was a true priest to me. Though nothing mystical happened on Samos I know somehow God was at work in me in Paul and in the schedules. Paul was so honest to me about what his career had meant to me. His very words were: "I think it came to something." I think so too. But often I have heard that God works in mysterious ways. Even with icons we do not see what we think we see. The icon is a window to the sacred. Was it just an accident that I came to know something of Paul Moore. Was it just serendipity? Often, I pray that Paul will watch over my life; my spirituality.

I must say that my wife wanted to help him and cared deeply when he died of cancer.

We married in July of 2004 and I heard the words so clear "God loves man and miracles happen." I believe my wife is a miracle. I believe Paul was a miracle.

Since my first unexplainable trip to Patmos, Greece I have been back two (2) more times. First, by myself; then with Bishop Moore and finally with my wife Provi. Each time I have been aware of miracles in my life. Not the least among these miracles has been the gift of life itself. Never do I regret the many letters I wrote when I was young to politicians opposing capital punishment. But even more joyfully I embrace the relationships I've had with those I've shared letters.

John the Apostle, said in his gospel: "God is Love." In my life it has been true that "Omnia Vincit Amor." I cannot repay the love my wife showed me when Bishop Moore was dying but it was love born of knowing what truly matters when cancer comes to take life. I barely survived when cancer took my father's life in 1983, My wife came into my life a survivor of cancer and Bishop Moore left from cancer at the same time. Life has shown me we are nothing without the love of at least one other human being. Many times love is poured forth in letters.

Paul Moore at the Cave of the Apocalypse in Patmos, Greece August 2002